Reptile rap

Bobbie Kalman

 Crabtree Publishing Company

www.crabtreebooks.com

Created by Bobbie Kalman

**Author and
Editor-in-Chief**
Bobbie Kalman

Reading consultant
Elaine Hurst

Editors
Kathy Middleton
Crystal Sikkens

Photo research
Bobbie Kalman

Design
Bobbie Kalman
Katherine Berti

**Production coordinator
and Prepress technician**
Katherine Berti

Photographs
BigStockPhoto: page 6 (bottom)
Other photographs by Shutterstock

Library and Archives Canada Cataloguing in Publication

Kalman, Bobbie, 1947-
   Reptile rap / Bobbie Kalman.

(My world)
ISBN 978-0-7787-9512-4 (bound).--ISBN 978-0-7787-9537-7 (pbk.)

   1. Reptiles--Juvenile literature. 2. Rap (Music)--Juvenile literature.
I. Title. II. Series: My world (St. Catharines, Ont.)

QL644.2.K23 2011   j597.9   C2010-902128-2

Library of Congress Cataloging-in-Publication Data

Kalman, Bobbie.
   Reptile rap / Bobbie Kalman.
      p. cm. -- (My world)
   ISBN 978-0-7787-9512-4 (reinforced lib. bdg. : alk. paper) --
   ISBN 978-0-7787-9537-7 (pbk. : alk. paper)
   1. Reptiles--Juvenile literature. 2. Rap (Music)--Juvenile literature.
I. Title. II. Series.

   QL644.2.K318 2011
   597.9--dc22
                                                    2010012531

Crabtree Publishing Company
www.crabtreebooks.com   1-800-387-7650

Printed in China/072010/AP20100226

**Published in Canada
Crabtree Publishing**
616 Welland Ave.
St. Catharines, Ontario
L2M 5V6

**Published in the United States
Crabtree Publishing**
PMB 59051
350 Fifth Avenue, 59th Floor
New York, New York 10118

**Published in the United Kingdom
Crabtree Publishing**
Maritime House
Basin Road North, Hove
BN41 1WR

**Published in Australia
Crabtree Publishing**
386 Mt. Alexander Rd.
Ascot Vale (Melbourne)
VIC 3032

Words to know

alligator

basking

crocodile

hatching

insect

lizard

scales

fangs

snake

tortoise

turtle

3

There are many kinds of **reptiles**. Some are big and some are small. How many of them do you know? Can you really name them all?

alligator

crocodile

Alligator, crocodile,
lizard, and snake.
How many rapping
reptiles does that make?
Don't forget the turtle,
for goodness' sake!

snake

lizard

turtle

"What are reptiles?"
you may be asking.
You might see reptiles
outside **basking**.

Basking is getting warm in the sun.
"Watch us bask to see how it's done.
Yeah! Basking in the sun is fun."

Our reptile skin
is covered in **scales**.
Scales cover us from
our heads to our tails.
As we grow bigger,
we shed our skin.
Our old skin falls off,
when new skin grows in.
"Yeah! We get new skin."

old skin

new skin

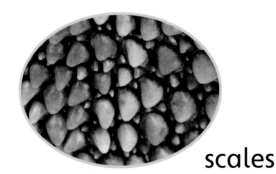

scales

Our mothers lay eggs
in a bunch
called a **batch**.
From these eggs,
we all soon **hatch**.

batch of
crocodile eggs

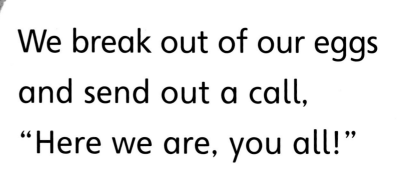

We break out of our eggs
and send out a call,
"Here we are, you all!"

8

When we are hungry and need to eat,
most of us like to eat some meat.
The taste of **insects** can't be beat!
Insects are animals with six legs and feet.

"This fly will taste yummy in my tummy!"

"We reptiles, called lizards,
all hatch from eggs.
We have long tails and very short legs."

"I am a gecko.
I have **pads**
on my feet."

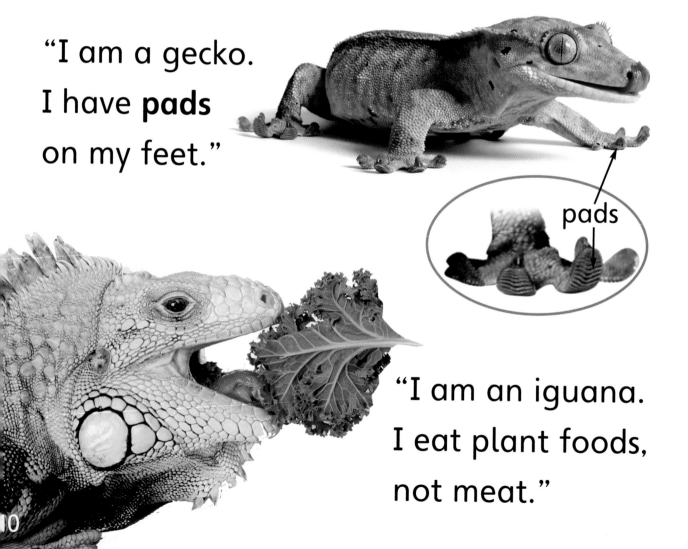

pads

"I am an iguana.
I eat plant foods,
not meat."

"I'm a colorful chameleon.
I change colors to show my mood."

"I'm a big
Komodo dragon.
I eat a lot of food!"

fangs

"We are snakes that **slither** and slide.
In grasses and trees we like to hide.
Some of us have **fangs** and **rattles**, too.
We shake our rattles loudly. We do, we do!"

rattle

slithering

12

"We are the biggest reptiles.
We're alligators and crocodiles.
We swim in water and run on land.
We like to sunbathe
on the sand."

crocodile

alligators

"We are part of one reptile group.
How can you tell?
    We are turtles and tortoises,
and we all have a shell!
Yeah! We all have a shell!"

tortoise

14

sea turtle

"Tortoises live on land,
but we turtles like water best.
Which of us have smaller shells?
Was it turtles that you guessed?
Some of us turtles live in the sea.
What are we called? Can you tell me?
Yeah! Can you please tell me?"

Notes for adults

Objectives
- to introduce children to animals called reptiles through rhyming rap verses and funny pictures
- to teach children about the different reptile groups in a fun way:
  1. alligators and crocodiles
  2. lizards and snakes
  3. turtles and tortoises
  (4. tuataras were left out at this level)

Before reading *Reptile rap*
Ask the children to read the books *Rodent rap* and *Hip-hop dancers.*

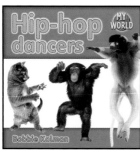

Guided Reading: E

Guided Reading: F

Rapping together
Read *Reptile rap*, line by line, to the class. Ask the children to repeat each line after you, keeping the rap beat. What other ways could they keep the beat?

Class discussion
Read each page spread again and discuss with the children these topics: the kinds of reptiles shown, why reptiles bask, what happens to their skin when reptiles grow, hatching from eggs, what reptiles eat, why chameleons change colors, how snakes move and why some have fangs and rattles, which are the biggest reptiles, and which reptiles have shells.

Hip-hopping, rapping fun!
Ask the children to make up their own rap verses about one or more reptiles. They can also perform reptile hip-hop dances. They can work on this activity in groups. Rapping is a fun way to introduce sounds and rhymes, as well as beat.

Who am I?
Play a game of "Who am I?" The children give clues by rapping about which reptile they are pretending to be. i.e. "I slither and shake. My name is…" or "I have a heavy shell. Who am I? Can you tell?"

For teacher's guide, go to www.crabtreebooks.com/teachersguides